CONTINENTS
OF THE WORLD

AUSTRALIA, OCEANIA AND ANTARCTICA

Kate Darian-Smith

First published in 2005 by Hodder Wayland,
an imprint of Hodder Children's Books

© Hodder Wayland 2005

Commissioning editor: Victoria Brooker
Editor: Katie Sergeant
Inside design: Jane Hawkins

Cover design: Hodder Wayland
Series concept and project management by
EASI-Educational Resourcing
(info@easi-er.co.uk) Statistical research: Anna Bowden

Population Density Map
© 2003 UT-Battelle, LLC. All rights reserved.
Data for population distribution maps reproduced under licence from UT-Battelle, LLC.
All rights reserved.

Maps and graphs: Martin Darlison, Encompass Graphics

British Library Cataloguing in Publication Data
Darian-Smith, Kate
  Australia, Oceania and Antarctica. – (Continents of the world)
  1. Australia, Oceania and Antarctica – Juvenile literature
  I.Title
  970
ISBN 0 7502 4680 4

Printed and bound in China

Hodder Children's Books
A division of Hodder Headline Limited
338 Euston Road, London NW1 3BH

Picture acknowledgements
The author and publisher would like to thank the following for allowing their
pictures to be reproduced in this publication:
Page 1 & 58: Reuters/Corbis; 3 & 6 and main cover: Owen Franken/Corbis; 5 Craig Tuttle/ Corbis; cover inset and
page 7 Mark A. Johnson/Corbis; 8 Science Photo Library; 9 Mary Evans Picture Library; 10 David
Mercado/Reuters/Corbis; 11 Mary Evans Picture Library;12 Bettmann/ Corbis;13 Bettmann/ Corbis; 14 Alamy; 15
NHPA/Ant Photo Library; 16 Dennis Degnan/Corbis; 17 Irfan Parvez/Alamy; 18 Doug Perrine / Still Pictures; 18
(bottom) Jay Dickman/Corbis; 20 Ed Chrisostomo/Corbis Sygma; 21 George D. Lepp/Corbis; 23 Paul A.
Souders/Corbis; 24: Penny Tweedie/Alamy; 25 Duomo/Corbis; 27 (top) Bob Krist/Corbis; (bottom)Wolfgang
Kaehler/ Corbis; 28 Ted Streshinsky/Corbis; 29 Reuters/Corbis; 30 Nik Wheeler/Corbis; 31 Sami Sarkis/Alamy; 32
Walter Bibikow/Alamy; 33 Christine Osborne Pictures; 34 The Art Archive/Musée des Arts Africains et Océaniens
/ Dagli Orti (A); 35 Manuel Blondeau/Photo & Co./Corbis; 36 Andy Christodolo/Alamy; 37 Wayne
Lawler/Ecoscene; 38 Doug Steley/Alamy; 39 Tim Graham/Alamy; 40 & 41 Friedrich Stark / Still Pictures; 42 Roger
Garwood & Trish Ainslie/Corbis; 43 Greg Smith/Corbis; 44 Catherine Karnow/Corbis; 45 Durocher
Christian/Corbis Sygma; main cover and 46 Bob Krist/Corbis; 47 Staffan Widstrand/Corbis; 48 Paul Thompson;
Eye Ubiquitous; 49 Reuters/Corbis; 50 Duomo/Corbis; 51 Reuters/Corbis; 52 Matthew McKee; Eye
Ubiquitous/Corbis; 53 Kevin Fleming/Corbis; 54 Martin Harvey/Corbis; 55 Jean Paul Ferrero/Ardea; 56 Paul A.
Souders/Corbis; 57 (top) Tim Davis/Corbis, (bottom) Jurgen Freud/Nature Picture Library; 59 The Image
Bank/Getty Images

Main cover picture: Western Samoa's Lalomanu Beach is typical of the island paradise that is attracting
increasing numbers of tourists to Oceania.

The website addresses (URLs) included in this book were valid at the time of
going to press. However, because of the nature of the Internet, it is possible that
some addresses may have changed, or sites may have changed or closed down
since publication. While the author and Publishers regret any inconvenience this
may cause the readers, no responsibility for any such changes can be accepted
by either the author or the Publisher.

The high volcanic peaks and coral-fringed beaches
of Bora Bora Island in French Polynesia.

CONTENTS

AUSTRALIA, OCEANIA AND ANTARCTICA: REGION OF DIVERSITY

Australia is the world's smallest continent, with a landmass of 7,686,850 sq km (2,967,124 sq miles). Australia's geographical remoteness has meant that it hosts many distinctive forms of animal and plant life. Much of the continent consists of low plateaus and arid deserts, but the majority of the population lives on the wetter, fertile plains in the south and east.

Antarctica is the world's fifth-largest continent and is located almost entirely within the Antarctic Circle, with the South Pole lying at its centre. It covers

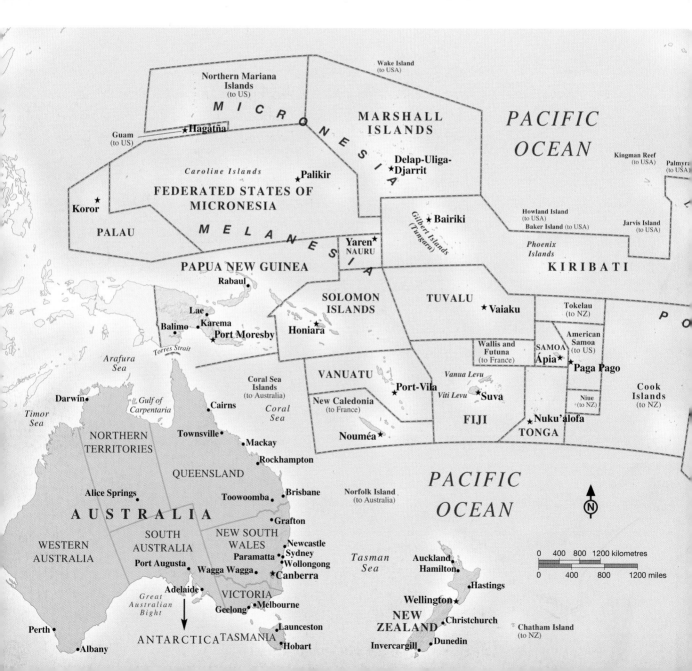

approximately 14,245,000 sq km (5,498,570 sq miles) of which only 5 per cent is ice-free. The remainder is overlain by a continental ice-sheet measuring approximately 30 million cubic kilometres (7.2 million cubic miles) and at places is over 2 kilometres (1.25 miles) thick. There is no permanent human habitation on Antarctica, although it is important as a scientific station.

East of Australia is the Pacific Ocean, the massive body of water between the Southern Ocean, Asia, Australia, and the western hemisphere. The Pacific Ocean contains some 25,000 islands. Ten thousand of these islands in the tropical and sub-tropical areas of the central and South Pacific Ocean are known collectively as Oceania.

The Oceanic islands are divided into three groups on the basis of their similarities and differences in geography, and the cultures of their peoples: Polynesia, Melanesia and Micronesia. A population of just 12.4 million people live on only 10 per cent of these scattered islands. The majority (58.4 per cent) are located in Melanesia, with 5.5 million located in Papua New Guinea alone.

Polynesia ('many islands') occupies a large part of the eastern Pacific Ocean between Hawaii, New Zealand and Easter Island. Its many thousands of islands range from large volcanic formations to tiny coral atolls, and are home to 4 million people or 38 per cent of the population of Oceania.

Micronesia ('tiny islands') comprises more than 2,000 low-lying and coral islands. Only 3.1 per cent of Oceania's population lives in Micronesia.

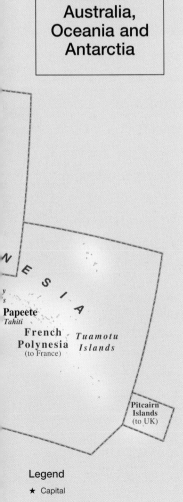

Political divisions in Australia, Oceania and Antarctia

N E S I A

y
s

Papeete
Tahiti
French Polynesia
(to France)
Tuamotu Islands

Pitcairn Islands
(to UK)

Legend

★ Capital

• Major settlement

The coral-fringed beaches of Bora Bora Island are typical of many small islands in Polynesia.

1. THE HISTORIES OF AUSTRALIA, OCEANIA AND ANTARCTICA

SOME 650-550 MILLION YEARS AGO, THE 'SUPERCONTINENT' Gondwanaland comprised all of the continents now located in the southern hemisphere: Australia, Antarctica, South America and Africa, as well as the Indian sub-continent. Gradually, Gondwanaland split up. A southern landmass with Australia at its core broke away some 45 million years ago, and began to drift northward. As ocean levels rose at the end of the last ice age (some 12 to 8 million years ago), land bridges between Australia and what are now Papua New Guinea and New Zealand were flooded over.

The high volcanic peaks and coral-fringed beaches of Bora Bora Island in French Polynesia.

THE FIRST INHABITANTS

The human histories of the region are complex and dynamic. According to archaeologists, Australia's indigenous peoples, the Aboriginal people, have the longest continuous cultural history in the world. Australia has been inhabited for at least 50,000-60,000 years. Scientists think that the first settlers travelled from South-east Asia by sea and over land bridges that connected Indonesia and New Guinea with Australia.

Parts of Melanesia were inhabited about 4,000 years ago by seafaring peoples from South-east Asia and from the Fujian province of southern China. They gradually travelled from Melanesia into Polynesia and Micronesia, settling on the islands. By c. AD 800,

Polynesian sea-farers, the ancestors of the Maori people, had reached New Zealand, and established communities largely on its North Island.

EUROPEAN EXPLORATION

From ancient times, European cultures speculated that a 'great southern continent' balanced the world. In AD 731 an English monk, the Venerable Bede, suggested that the poles were regions of eternal cold, and while the North Pole was ocean, the South Pole was a great land. In 1366, Sir John Mandeville, an English author of travellers' tales, was the first to use the word 'Antarktyk' ('opposite the Arctic').

Between the fifteenth and seventeenth centuries, interest in the existence of a 'great south land' was heightened by the

●●●●●●▶ IN FOCUS: Easter Island

On Easter Island, in the Pacific Ocean, about 600 enormous stone statues and platforms, known as Moais, were carved from volcanic rock between AD 400 and 1600. Archaeologists are unsure what these monuments represented, but they believe they were erected by different tribes competing for land. The largest of the Moais is 12 metres (39 feet) tall. It would probably take about 100 people to move each Moais from the quarry where it was carved to its final resting place.

The Easter Island statues are thought by some scholars to represent the spirits of ancient chiefs and other important men.

7

FACT FILE

Captain Cook landed at Botany Bay, near present-day Sydney, in 1770. He claimed possession of the eastern half of the continent for Britain, naming it New South Wales.

competition between the sea-going European powers to 'discover' new parts of the world. European explorers had already reached the Americas and Asia when sailors from Spain, Portugal, Britain and France ventured farther into unchartered southern seas. In 1606, the Dutch explorer Willem Jansz sighted northern Australia. In 1642, another Dutchman, Abel Tasman, was the first to sight New Zealand, but hostility from the native people at Golden Bay, in the northeastern corner of New Zealand's South Island, prevented him from landing.

The most famous European explorer in the Pacific was an Englishman – Captain James Cook. His voyages mapped much of Melanesia and Polynesia, as well as the east coast of Australia. In 1768 Cook was sent by the British government to the island of Tahiti (now in French Polynesia) to view the transit of the planet Venus, and then to explore the southern Pacific. In two further voyages, Cook made a circuit of the Pacific region south of the Equator, and established that New South Wales was, in fact, part of the continent of Australia.

EUROPEAN COLONIZATION IN AUSTRALIA AND OCEANIA

A British penal colony was established at Sydney Cove in New South Wales in 1788. The First Fleet carrying convicts and government officers sailed on an eight-month journey from England, and the group endured hardship due to lack of adequate food supplies in the first years at the settlement. The practice of transporting convicts to Australia continued until the 1840s in the eastern colonies and 1868 in Western Australia. It was not long, however, until 'free immigrants' began to arrive. They were

Captain James Cook sailed in the *Endeavour* on his voyage of discovery in 1768-1771.

drawn by the promise of land, and, by the 1850s, the discovery of gold.

As well as New South Wales, the separate British colonies of Tasmania, Victoria, South Australia, Western Australia and Queensland were established on the Australian continent. The British claimed that they had a right to the land under the legal doctrine of *terra nullius* ('uninhabited land'), despite the presence of Aboriginal peoples. Aboriginal peoples were driven from their traditional territories and there were many violent clashes between them and the settlers.

After 1790 European settlements were founded in New Zealand by whalers, who first came from bases in Australia, and later came directly from Britain, France and the United States. They were after products such as sealskin, timber, flax (a plant used to make linen) and whale oil. By 1840 the British government took possession of New Zealand to protect the interests of British whalers and sealers. British immigration to New Zealand grew, and towns sprang up. Tensions with Maori, the indigenous landowners, quickly escalated into land wars in the 1850s and 1860s, resulting in the defeat of the indigenous peoples.

By the early 19th century, the European presence in Oceania was permanent. Political and territorial tensions in Europe contributed to the histories of the British, French and German colonization. Traders and those who established

FACT FILE

Many Aboriginal people died because they had no immunity to diseases introduced by European settlers, such as measles, smallpox and even the common cold.

In 1835 settler John Batman offered a treaty to the Aboriginal owners of the site where the city of Melbourne was to be built. This treaty is not recognised as having any legal standing.

plantations for tropical crops often preceded the formal territorial claims of European governments. There was a European scramble for the colonial possession of many of the Oceanic islands, and some islands have experienced successive waves of foreign colonization.

Britain took over many areas of interest in Oceania, including Fiji, the Solomon Islands and a number of other smaller island groups. The French annexed various Polynesian island groups, including New Caledonia, Wallis and Futuna and French Polynesia. In 1898 Germany purchased the islands of what is now the modern nation of the Federated States of Micronesia from their previous colonial power, Spain. These islands were to come under Japanese control in 1914.

Since 1828 the western half of New Guinea had been in the hands of the Dutch, and remained so until 1963 when the United Nations sanctioned its transfer to Indonesia. In 1884 a German-owned trading company moved into the northeastern part of New Guinea. In reaction to this settlement, Britain and its Australian colonies seized Papua in the southeast part of the island. British New Guinea became an Australian territory in 1901, and from 1920 German New Guinea was also under Australian rule. Indeed, until its independence in 1975, an amalgamated Papua New Guinea was administered by Australia.

In 1820 American missionaries arrived in Hawaii, and were soon followed by whalers and settlers. The Hawaiian monarchy was overturned in the early 1890s by American

Sir Michael Somare was Papua New Guinea's first Prime Minister after independence in 1975, and has served three terms as Prime Minister.

sugar planters. Hawaii was annexed by the United States in 1898, became a US territory in 1900, and a state in 1959. The US naval base at Pearl Harbor was established in 1908. By 1900, after a short war with Spain, the United States assumed control of Guam and other previous Spanish possessions in the islands of Micronesia.

INDEPENDENCE

In 1901 the separate British colonies in Australia federated to become one nation. The new Australia maintained the British monarch as its symbolic head of government, and adopted the

●●●●●●➤ IN FOCUS: Treaty of Waitangi

This Treaty was regarded as the 'founding document of New Zealand', and was signed in 1840 by 500 Maori chiefs and a representative of the British government. However the treaty was never officially approved by the British parliament and had no legal validity. The British and Maori versions were completely contradictory. The Waitangi Tribunal was established in 1976 to consider disputes relating to the treaty. By 2003 there had been 18 settlements of historical treaty claims from Maori people, worth a total value of almost US$430 million. Access to traditional food sources, including fishing rights, have now been returned to the Maori, and they have received property and cash in compensation for the loss of their land.

The Treaty of Waitangi was signed by 500 Maori chiefs on 21 May 1840.

11

British system of parliament with an upper and lower house. New Zealand was declared an independent Dominion of the British Empire in 1907.

From the 1960s most of the island-nations of Oceania have gained some degree of political autonomy from the five foreign nations that administered them – the United Kingdom, France, the United States, Australia and New Zealand. France and the United States have been the most resistant to support independence, largely due to their military interests in the Oceanic region.

WAR IN THE PACIFIC

The recent histories of some societies in Oceania have been influenced by fighting in the Pacific during World War II, as contact with American and Australian troops influenced cultural and economic developments through exposure to Western attitudes and commodities. The Japanese bombing of the United States' naval base at Pearl Harbor in Hawaii on 7 December 1941 brought the United States' forces into World War II. Under the command of US General Douglas MacArthur, US, Australian and New Zealand troops fought

US forces liberated the North Mariana island of Saipan from the Japanese on 28 June 1944.

against the Japanese on some Oceanic islands, including Papua New Guinea, the Mariana Islands, Guam and Kiribati. The decisive Battles of the Coral Sea (4-8 May 1942) and Midway Island (3-6 June 1942), when US forces repelled Japanese troops, took place in the Pacific.

ANTARCTIC EXPLORATION

From the early nineteenth century various British, French and American expeditions surveyed the frozen continent of Antarctica. The struggle inland to reach the geographic South Pole began with the 1901 expedition of Britain's Robert F. Scott. In January 1909 Australian Douglas Mawson reached the magnetic South Pole by sledge, while a Norwegian expedition led by Roald Amundsen and Thorvald Nilsen was the first to reach the geographic South Pole on 14 December 1911. Scott and his companions arrived a month later, but perished in a severe blizzard on their journey back to their base camp.

By the 1950s expeditions to Antarctica were marked by international rivalry, resulting in the establishment of permanent scientific stations across Antarctica. In 1959, twelve nations with territorial interests in Antarctica, including Argentina, Australia, Chile, France, New Zealand, Norway and the UK, signed the Antarctica Treaty. This treaty set up a legal framework for the management of Antarctica. It permits scientific inquiry and forbids military operations or nuclear testing. Many other nations are now formally consulted about Antarctica's future.

FACT FILE

On 7 February 1821 the American Captain John Davis became the first known person to land on Antarctica.

The Norwegian explorers Roald Amundsen and Thorvald Nilsen check their bearings to confirm they've reached the South Pole.

2. AUSTRALIAN, OCEANIC AND ANTARCTIC ENVIRONMENTS

*T*OGETHER AUSTRALIA, ANTARCTICA AND OCEANIA COVER massive land and sea areas and encompass extraordinarily diverse and extreme environmental conditions. Antarctica's frozen plateaus contrast with the balmy tropics of the Pacific. Australia's water-starved and barren deserts stand out against its lush tropical rainforests. The coral atolls of the Pacific Islands belie the region's volcanic mountains, which are often hidden by low-lying clouds.

Dead fish at Australia's Lake Eyre after its waters have dried up.

FACT FILE

Although Antarctica is the driest continent, Australia is the driest inhabited continent in the world.

AUSTRALIA: 'THE DRY CONTINENT'

The landmass of Australia extends over 33° of latitude, one third of which lies between the Equator and the Tropic of Capricorn. It is an ancient land, with some rock formations dating back at least 3,000 million years.

More than 60 per cent of Australia's terrain is dominated by arid to semi-arid low plateaus and great deserts. In these areas the average annual rainfall is less than 300 mm (12 inches). The lowest rainfall recorded is at Lake Eyre with less than 150 mm per annum (6 inches). Lake Eyre is generally a dry saltpan, and is only filled with water every few years.

The highest temperature ever recorded in Australia of 52.7° Celsius (127° Fahrenheit) was in 1889 at Cloncurry, in inland Queensland. The lowest temperature of –19°C (–3° F) was recorded at Charlotte Pass, in the Snowy

The Murray-Darling system is a major waterway that stretches over 3,700 kilometres (2,300 miles) from Queensland to South Australia. The Murray River flows from the Snowy Mountains to the Great Australian Bight in South Australia. Its main tributaries are the Darling, Murrumbidgee and Goulburn Rivers. The 'mighty' Murray passes through Australia's main wheat and sheep producing regions, as well as irrigation areas where cotton, rice, citrus fruits, and grapes are grown. The Murray River also provides the water needs of many towns, as well as the city of Adelaide. The overuse of water in the Murray-Darling river system has damaged the habitation of waterbirds, wetlands and flood plains. It has also resulted in increasing salinity within the soil. But farming along the Murray supports dozens of small towns, thousands of jobs and an economy worth millions of dollars. The Murray-Darling Basin Commission has been established by the government to manage the use of Australia's major river system, and to examine how environmental sustainability can be achieved.

The Murray River originates in Australia's spectacular Snowy Mountains.

Mountains. Droughts occur regularly in Australia, as do flash floods that follow periods of sudden and heavy rain.

Australia's red and yellow-brown sandy soiled deserts host a vegetation of spinifex, cane grass and saltbushes, and are the home of animals and insect life acclimatized to the extreme temperatures and arid conditions, such as snakes, termites and lizards including large goannas. At the edges of the desert are semi-arid areas of mallee (dwarf eucalyptus) and mulga (acacia) scrub. Here the tree forms are bushy with

FACT FILE

The Gibson Desert, Great Victorian Desert, Great Sandy Desert and Nullarbor Plain are Australia's largest deserts and together spread across large parts of Western Australia, South Australia and the Northern Territory.

many branching trunks that may form a dense canopy that protects rodents, such as jerba-rats, small hare-wallabies, rat-kangaroos and reptiles, from large predators.

The central highlands regions in the eastern and northern parts of Australia make up more than a quarter of the continent. Here the flat, semi-arid scrub gives way to mountain ranges and savannah grasslands. Annual seasonal rains produce carpets of multi-coloured annual flowers and herbs.

The highland region of the eastern coastline makes up 15 per cent of Australia and is dominated by the Great Dividing Range of mountains. The climate ranges from temperate in the southern half of the highland region to tropical in the northern half. The tropical north also receives the highest rainfalls. The wettest recorded location in Australia is Tully in Northern Queensland with an average rainfall of 4,300 mm (170 inches).

Sixty per cent of Australia relies on ground water such as lakes, pools and runoff, and underground water, particularly the Great Artesian Basin. The Basin stretches through Queensland to South Australia and is the largest body of underground water in the world. However, overuse, particularly for livestock watering, has greatly exceeded natural replenishment through its internal drainage system, causing the level of the Basin to drop. As a consequence many bores, or wells, have run dry or require pumping. These issues are being addressed through conservation efforts.

Millaa Millaa Falls are located in northern Queensland, and are a popular site for swimming.

THE ISLANDS OF OCEANIA

Oceania's islands have a variety of landforms, soils, and plant and animal life. They are divided into continental and oceanic islands.

Continental islands are largely high mountainous islands with rich soils, located on the now partly submerged continental shelf that stretches along the western Pacific Ocean and that links Asia and Australia. This shelf covers 885,780 sq km (342,000 sq miles) and measures 2,415 km (1,500 miles) long and 645 km (400 miles) at its widest. New Guinea's vast mountain ranges such as the Owen Stanley and Bismarck mountains are about 5,000 metres (16,400 feet) high and are snow-capped, while the low coastal plains are either swampy or densely forested. New Zealand is also predominantly mountainous with some coastal plains. Its highest mountain is Aoraki-Mount Cook at 3,754 metres (12,316 feet).

Oceanic islands are split between the high, volcanic islands of Polynesia and Micronesia, and low coral atolls with reefs that make up the majority of Pacific Islands. On these coral islands, which have been built up by coral reef deposits over millions of years, the lowest point is often at sea level. These islands contrast strongly with the dense, basalt volcanic outcroppings that rise thousands of

New Zealand's Aoraki-Mount Cook National Park on the South Island was declared a National Park in 1953.

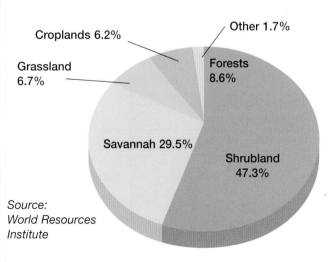

Habitat and land use in Oceania and Australia.

Croplands 6.2%
Grassland 6.7%
Savannah 29.5%
Other 1.7%
Forests 8.6%
Shrubland 47.3%

Source: World Resources Institute

17

FACT FILE

Mauna Kea in Hawaii is the highest island mountain in the world, rising 9,760 metres (32,021 feet) from the Pacific Ocean floor, and 4,208 metres (13,796 feet) above sea level.

Hawaii's snow-capped Mauna Kea is a dormant volcano that last erupted 4,000 years ago.

metres out of the sea, such as French Polynesia's Mont Orohena (2,241 metres/7,352 feet) or Hawaii's now dormant, snow-capped Mauna Kea.

The islands on the Continental plateau generally are more fertile than volcanic or coral ocean islands. Over time, their size, geological age and climate have combined to enrich the soil with nutrients and minerals. However, the amount of productive land is limited due to their mountain ranges and usually is found on the lower mountain slopes or alluvial plains. Fiji, for example, is 18,270 sq km (7,052 sq miles) in size but only 12 per cent is arable land.

Coral islands suffer other limitations too. One is their small size. Another is the leaching of nutrients by heavy rainfall, reducing the fertility of the soil. Farmers are forced to use fertilizers or leave the land unused for a long period of time to allow the soil to regenerate. Associated environmental problems include soil erosion, which has been hastened by rapid deforestation, as is occurring in the Solomon Islands.

Many economies of Oceania have been forced to seek revenue through the introduction of industries that damage the environment, such as the cutting down of forests.

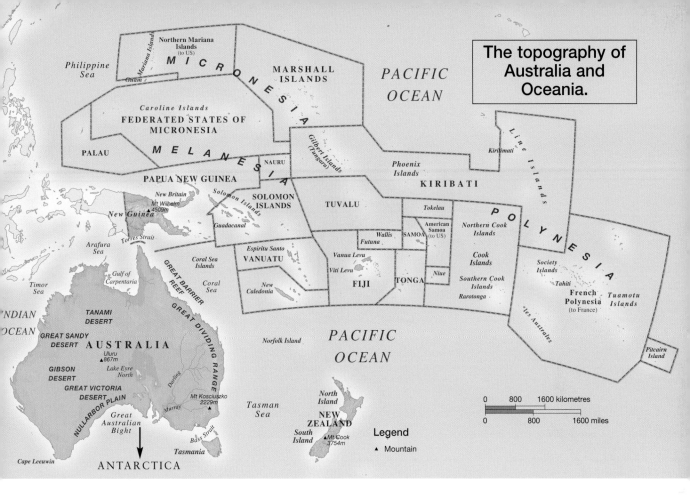

The topography of Australia and Oceania.

Another problem facing most islands is the lack of fresh water. Despite high rainfalls most do not have large catchment areas to retain fresh water. It means that governments, like American Samoa, have to invest a lot of money improving water catchment and pipelines.

CLIMATE IN OCEANIA

The climate of Oceania is uniformly tropical with high humidity and heavy rainfall all year round. The regional differences that occur are the result of altitude, air circulation patterns and the time of the year. Therefore during November to March, islands such as the Solomon Islands and New Guinea receive monsoonal rains on their western slopes carried by the northwest monsoon from Asia, while in summer the southeast monsoon brings rain to the eastern slopes.

FACT FILE

The mountainous island of New Guinea is the world's second-largest island after Greenland.

Typhoons, such as the one that struck Guam in 1997, regularly leave devastation in their wake.

Seasonal weather is also responsible for the typhoons or hurricanes that often occur in western Micronesia from July to November. These storms bring severe winds, torrential rain and high waves. They cause extensive damage to crops and buildings especially on low-lying coral islands.

EL NIÑO

The most destructive climatic phenomenon in the region is El Niño. It is a disruption of the ocean-atmosphere system that occurs in the tropical Pacific Ocean, but which has consequences on climatic conditions globally. During El Niño, the trade winds in the central and western Pacific lose their strength, resulting in an unusual rise in the temperature of the ocean, and irregular patterns of rainfall and atmospheric currents. As a consequence, marine life is affected, and the atmospheric changes can cause destructive storms and hurricanes in the Pacific, and severe drought in parts of Australia.

FACT FILE

The mountain ranges of Antarctica have altitudes of over 4,500 metres (14,764 feet).

ANTARCTICA

Antarctica is the highest continent on earth, with an average land height of 2,000 metres (6,560 feet). The highest mountain is Vinson Massif at 4,897 metres (16,066 feet). In contrast, the lowest known land point is hidden in the Bentley Subglacial Trench, at 2,555 metres (8,382 feet) below sea level. This is the deepest ice yet discovered and the world's lowest elevation not under seawater.

The Circum-Antarctic Current is the world's largest ocean current. It circulates clockwise around the entire Antarctic continent and is associated with a system of prevailing westerly winds that encircle the globe at latitudes between 40 and 60 degrees, known as the Roaring Forties, Furious Fifties and Screaming Sixties.

Antarctica is the coldest, windiest, highest and driest continent on Earth. The lowest temperature ever recorded on Earth is –89.4 °C (–129 °F) in 1983 at Vostok. The strongest winds have been recorded at 375 kilometres per hour (233 mph) at D'Urville. The average rainfall that falls on the polar plateau is less than 50 mm (2 inches) per year.

During summer in the southern hemisphere, the South Pole receives more direct solar radiation from the Sun than anywhere else on the planet. As a consequence, the greatest environmental threat to Antarctica is the ozone hole covering the region, which in 1998 was identified by NASA as the largest on record, covering 27 million sq km (10 million sq miles). The ultraviolet light coming through the hole is damaging ice-fish, marine plants and causing the disintegration of significant areas of ice shelves.

The Alimirante Brown research station at Pacific Bay in Antarctica is maintained by Argentina.

3. THE PEOPLES OF AUSTRALIA, OCEANIA AND ANTARCTICA

*A*N ESTIMATED 32.4 MILLION PEOPLE LIVE AND WORK IN AUSTRALIA, OCEANIA and Antarctica. The majority are of European descent, and their migration to the region over the past two centuries has dramatically altered its ethnic and cultural profile. Australia and New Zealand, as former settler colonies of Britain, have been the leading destinations for millions of migrants from Britain, and increasingly from other parts of Europe, Asia and the United States. However, recent decades have also seen an increased pattern of internal migration within the region itself.

AUSTRALIA'S PEOPLE

Australia's population is around 20 million. During the first 150 years of colonial settlement, about 98 per cent of immigrants came from the British Isles, with a large proportion from Ireland. However, the goldrush

FACT FILE

Antarctica has no permanent inhabitants. However, approximately 4,000 scientists and support staff and naval crews stay there for limited periods of time throughout the year.

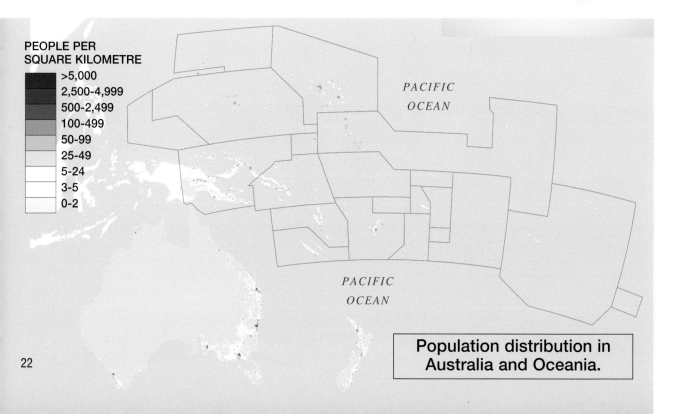

PEOPLE PER SQUARE KILOMETRE
- >5,000
- 2,500-4,999
- 500-2,499
- 100-499
- 50-99
- 25-49
- 5-24
- 3-5
- 0-2

PACIFIC OCEAN

PACIFIC OCEAN

Population distribution in Australia and Oceania.

of the 1850s attracted thousands of miners from China, as well as from many parts of Europe and the United States. In 1947, with a population of just 7 million, Australia launched a massive immigration program to boost its population numbers so as to aid economic development. In succeeding decades waves of migrants have arrived from northern, central and southern Europe, the Middle East, and, more recently, from Asia, particularly Vietnam and China. Australia's discriminatory 'White Australia' immigration policy, passed by federal legislation in 1901, was formally abandoned in 1973. The policy aimed to stop the immigration of non-Europeans to Australia through bureaucratic means. An official policy of multiculturalism has now been adopted, which recognizes the value of cultural diversity.

Children of Melbourne's large Greek community are dressed in traditional national costume to celebrate Greek Independence Day (25 March).

In 2004 almost 25 per cent of the Australian population was born overseas. Australia is, proportionally, second only to Israel in terms of being an 'immigrant nation'. While English remains the official language, more than 100 other languages are spoken in Australian homes. The city of Melbourne has the third largest Greek-speaking population in the world, outside Athens and Thessaloniki. Ethnic social clubs, places of worship, and shops are found in all Australian cities. About 7 per cent of the population is of Asian origin, and this proportion is rising.

However, the largest group of migrants to Australia in recent years – almost 20 per cent annually – have come from Oceania, primarily from New Zealand. Australia remains committed to admitting migrants under particular schemes, such as family reunion, and the preference for migrants with occupation or business skills that are seen to meet national interests. While Australia also supports the immigration of refugees on humanitarian grounds, there have been recent measures to deter those entering the country illegally, including holding illegal migrants or refugees in detention centres until their applications for migration can be officially processed. The Australian government has also not recognized many recent claims for refugee status made by potential migrants.

INDIGENOUS PEOPLES IN AUSTRALIA

Australia has two groups of indigenous peoples: Aboriginal peoples who live on the Australian mainland and in Tasmania, and Torres Strait Islanders whose traditional lands are in the islands of Torres Strait off the Cape York Peninsula in northern Australia. It is estimated that before European colonization, the indigenous populations numbered between 750,000 and 3 million. They occupied about 500 different territories and spoke hundreds of distinct languages, although the majority of these have now disappeared.

Todd Conde, pictured here with his mother Lismore, is editor of the national newspaper for Aboriginal and Torres Strait Islander people, the 'Koori Mail'.

In 1967, Aboriginal and Torres Strait Islander peoples were granted the same citizenship rights as other Australians. Land rights has become a major political issue, and some lands have been 'returned' to Aboriginal peoples. In 1992, a High Court decision overturned the concept of *terra nullius*, under which the British had settled in Australia. Aboriginal communities must now provide evidence of their prior occupation of the land, and the legal processes are complex. Many Aboriginal communities living in remote areas, however, now enjoy some degree of economic independence. Many other Aboriginal people live in Australia's cities and towns.

The 2001 national census figures show that the indigenous population in Australia number about 2.5 per cent (approximately 458,500), but the numbers are rising. The birth rate of indigenous peoples is higher than that of other Australians, but the average age of mortality is noticeably lower with health among the Aboriginal population being a major social issue. Sadly, the death rate of Australia's indigenous people is double that of non-indigenous people, and their average life expectancy is approximately 20 years lower than that for the non-indigenous population. The main health concerns of indigenous people are related to issues of poverty and inadequate healthcare services, particularly in rural areas.

Cathy Freeman, an Indigenous Australian athlete, won international acclaim after winning a gold medal at the Sydney Olympics in 2000.

New Zealand's Peoples

In 2004, approximately 79.1 per cent of the 4 million New Zealanders were of European – predominantly British – descent (referred to by the Maori as 'Pakeha'), representing the largest European settlement in Oceania. The Maori make up 9.7 per cent, 3.8 per cent are Pacific Islanders, and 7.4 per cent are Asian.

FACT FILE

The official bilingual name of New Zealand is 'New Zealand/Aotearoa'. 'Aotearoa' is the Maori name for the nation, and means 'land of the long white cloud'. The country's official emblem is the kiwi bird.

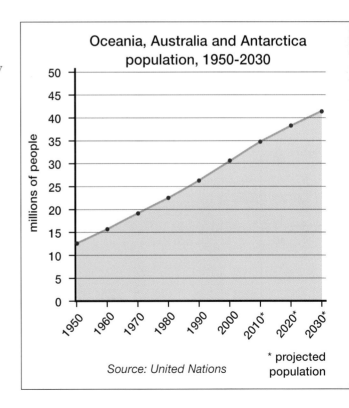

Oceania, Australia and Antarctica population, 1950-2030

millions of people

Source: United Nations

* projected population

New Zealand has adopted a policy of biculturalism, with both English and Maori as the official languages and Maori now being taught in schools. In 1769, the year of first European contact in New Zealand, there were about 200,000 Maori. By 1896 European colonization had reduced their numbers to 42,000, but since the middle of the twentieth century, that number has increased considerably to about 390,000 people in 2004.

URBAN NATIONS

Both Australia and New Zealand are highly urbanized nations. For over a century, people have drifted from rural areas to the cities for employment, education and economic reasons. Approximately 88 per cent of the Australian population now lives in cities and large towns. The cities on the eastern seaboard – Brisbane, Sydney, and Melbourne – account for almost half of the national population. Eighty per cent of New Zealanders also live in the country's cities and towns. Both Australian and New Zealand cities are distinguished by the continuing spread of their suburbs.

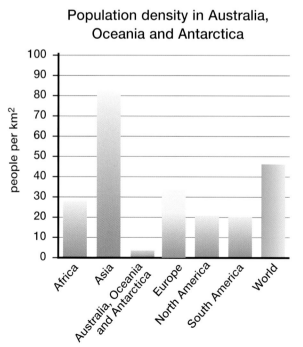

Population density in Australia, Oceania and Antarctica

The depopulation of rural areas in Australia has resulted in the loss of services such as banks and medical clinics in some towns. However, this trend may be reversing. The fastest growing regions in Australia are smaller, commuter and 'lifestyle' towns along the coast and inland from the major cities. The foreign ownership of land in Australia and New Zealand, especially along the coastline, has become a concern for local populations. Maori communities, for example, fear that this will lead to the loss of their access to traditional lands.

Source: United Nations; Britannica Book of the Year 2004

OCEANIA'S PEOPLES

The peoples who live in the Oceanic groups of Micronesia, Melanesia and Polynesia are enormously diverse in their cultures. Indeed, 1,200 of the world's 6,800 languages are spoken by the 7 million people who live in Oceania. New Guinea alone has 715 indigenous languages, while Polynesia has 20 and Micronesia another thirteen.

The marrow of the sago palm-tree is a staple part of the diet of villagers of Papua New Guinea.

The largest indigenous populations are in Melanesia, particularly on Papua New Guinea (approximately 5.4 million), Fiji (approximately 900,000) and Solomon Islands (approximately 523,000). Polynesia has the second largest population (approximately 684,000, excluding Hawaii). The Polynesian people, as well as the Micronesian population, are dispersed over many islands, with the number of people on each island varying from a few hundred to tens of thousands. The 21,000 inhabitants of the Cook Islands, for example, are dispersed over seven low-lying, infertile, and sparsely populated coral atolls, and eight volcanic islands which support the majority of people.

FACT FILE

Pitcairn Island has the smallest population in Oceania with a population of around 50 people. The population has declined due to the lack of fresh water and the need for people to leave the island for work or study.

Most Oceanic islanders continue to live in rural and fishing communities, often in small villages with limited opportunities for employment. The rising

Net fishing in shallow waters is a primary source of food for many Micronesian villagers.

FACT FILE

More people from the Cook Islands and Niue actually live in New Zealand than in their own countries.

population growth rate in many Oceanic nations (between 1-2 per cent each year) has caused serious issues of overpopulation. For example, Kiribati's 100,800 people are spread over 21 of the 33 small coral atolls and place a strain on the few available resources.

The limitations of space, resources and employment have meant that increasing numbers of people within Oceania are moving to urban centres, or migrating to New Zealand and the French and United States-controlled nations.

Immigration and settlement from Europe, Asia and the United States have changed the demographic profile of many Oceanic island-nations. Besides residents with European ancestry, Hawaii has a large number of immigrants from the US mainland, China, Japan, Korea and the Philippines. New Caledonia has had an influx of French as well Chinese, Vietnamese and Indonesian migrants. In Fiji, 44 per cent of the population of 900,000 are Indo-Fijian. These are descendants of indentured labourers from the Indian sub-continent who were brought to Fiji during the colonial period to work on the sugar plantations.

Hawaii's cultural diversity is seen in this Buddhist temple that was converted into a museum in 1985.

EDUCATION IN THE REGION

Australia and New Zealand have education systems of equal standard to those in other Western, developed nations. Their university systems are internationally acclaimed and attract many students from Asia, the United States and the Oceanic region.

Educational opportunities in some Oceanic nations are limited. Overall, however, literacy levels are improving, and regional higher education institutions (for example the multi-campus University of the South Pacific) have played an important role in providing professional training.

FACT FILE

Eighty per cent of Australian high school students enroll in higher education at universities or colleges. This level of higher education is only surpassed in the United States and Canada.

IN FOCUS: Fiji

Conflict between different ethnic groups has led to political and economic instability in Fiji. In 1970 Fiji gained independence from Britain but remained a member of the British Commonwealth. In 1987 Sitiveni Rabuka, a colonel in the Fijian army, led two military coups against the government, which was dominated by Fijians of Indian descent (Indo-Fijians). He proclaimed Fiji a republic, severing ties to the Commonwealth. By early 1988 the country returned to civilian rule, but violence and tension between Fijians and Indo-Fijians continued. On 19 May 2000 a civilian coup was executed by radical indigenous Fijians who ousted Fiji's first ethnic Indian government led by Prime Minister Chaudry. Indigenous

Fijians were concerned about proposed land reforms and possible social justice laws. In 2004 Indo-Fijians continue to be denied a share of the political power and suffer social, economic and educational discrimination. The government has attempted to heal the political and racial instability by calling for national prayer meetings involving the Christian, Hindu and Muslim populations, and public demonstrations of patriotism such as flag flying.

Fijian nationalists march on Parliament House in May 2000 to show support for the military coup.

4. CULTURE AND RELIGION IN AUSTRALIA AND OCEANIA

MIGRATION AND SETTLEMENT FROM EUROPE AND THE UNITED **States into Australia and Oceania have deeply influenced the cultural, religious and social facets of traditional life in the region.**

THE MISSIONARIES AND CHRISTIANITY

The preaching of evangelical Protestant and Roman Catholic missionaries among Oceanic peoples began in 1798, when the London Missionary Society first arrived on Tahiti. As a result of continued evangelical efforts, Christianity has become the dominant religion in Oceania. Almost the entire population of Western Samoa, for example, is officially Christian. In some cases, there has been development of localized Christian denominations, as in the Cook Islands Christian Church.

The influence of missionaries and European settlers brought about changes in the traditional lifestyles of people in Oceania, such as alternative agricultural methods and the introduction of Western clothing. However, in many cases traditional beliefs and kinship systems have been integrated into Westernized forms of social, political and economic life.

TRADITIONAL BELIEFS IN OCEANIA

Traditional lifestyles, religions and societies in the island-nations of Oceania are very diverse. In general terms, Oceanic religions worshipped many gods, and

Christianity is widely practised in Oceania, and churches like this one on the Cook Islands are numerous.

these beliefs are present in everyday activities and artistic practices. A close relationship existed between the living and the spirits of ancestors.

Oceanic mythology was passed down by oral tradition through many generations. Their complex stories tell of gods and spirits who are linked to places of symbolic significance. Adaro, the sea spirit, appears in many Polynesian and Melanesian myths. Some myths explain the existence of the sea as the sweat of the spiritual parent and god of the oceans, Tangaroa, as he created the world.

In some places in Melanesia, traditional religious beliefs are still practised.

Kinship in Oceania

The ties that link the individual, the family and the community are known as kinship relationships. These are extremely important in traditional Oceanic cultures, and determine all political and social structures. Kinship relationships are often maintained through exchange of foodstuffs and tokens such as shells and beads and feathers, and are marked by ritual ceremonies.

In many societies, there is a strict hierarchy based on birthright and political importance. In Polynesian and Micronesian societies, the position of chief is inherited, and it is supported through *mana* or personal power. A number of modern independent Polynesian states only permit those who are chiefs to hold positions in parliament. In Tonga, civil war broke out following the arrival of British missionaries. In 1845, a strong chief united the people and was crowned King, establishing a hereditary monarchy.

FACT FILE

Despite being firmly tied to the United States, in the Federated States of Micronesia men wear loincloths and still use stone coins as currency, while ties and baseball caps have been banned.

FACT FILE

Tonga has the only constitutional monarchy in Oceania.

ARTISTIC LIFE IN OCEANIA

In some traditions the sea god Tangaroa had human children, one of whom, Rua-te-pupuke, is said to have discovered the art of carving, a skill that became central to Oceanic culture. Art in Oceania is not produced for the sake of art itself, but for a particular political, social or religious function, such as the appeasement of gods or spirits. Oceanic visual art makes use of a great range of common-place materials found in the natural environment. The materials, the final product and the symbolic decorations vary enormously from community to community. Thus masks are worn in Melanesia but not Micronesia. Another medium for Oceanic art is the human body. The bluish-black tattoos worn by men and women in Polynesia, and to a lesser degree in Micronesia and Melanesia, announce physical maturity or prowess in battle.

Ritual body tattooing shows elaborate and complex designs.

Ornaments such as necklaces, ear and nose rings, leg and arm bands, made from shell, bone, whales' and other fish teeth, further mark out an individual's rank and wealth. Among Melanesian and Polynesian men, clamshell and turtle shell disks are worn as a necklace pendant or on a band around the forehead. In New Zealand coloured feathers are woven into cloaks worn by men and women of high tribal rank.

STORY-TELLING AND LITERATURE IN OCEANIA

Throughout Oceania, story-telling is very important and histories and other stories are told through oral traditions. There is a strong focus on song and dance as a means of

FACT FILE

In Papua New Guinea, feathers of the amazingly coloured birds of paradise are used as ceremonial decorations.

telling stories. In Melanesia, for example, dancers wearing elaborate costumes and masks describe the activities of gods and ancestors.

Traditional Oceanic societies had no written language. Today, there are written versions of the major languages, and English is widely taught in the school system. It was in the 1970s and 1980s that a 'Pacific' literature, written in English, began to be published. Writers such as Samoa's Albert Wendt have achieved recognition for fictional works that blend traditional forms of story-telling with an exploration of contemporary society.

RELIGION IN AUSTRALIA AND NEW ZEALAND

In Australia, Christianity remains the predominant religious group and represents approximately 76 per cent of the population. Islam is the fastest growing religion, reflecting the recent trend of immigration from the Middle East and parts of Asia. In New Zealand the various Christian denominations (especially Anglicanism and Presbyterianism) account for 64 per cent of religious belief.

THE ABORIGINAL DREAMTIME

Traditional Aboriginal society has a complex system of social, spiritual and cultural laws that are connected to their land. They believe that the creation of the world occurred during the Dreamtime, when ancestral spirits brought all plants, animals, rivers and mountains into existence. These Dreamtime creation stories are

Islam is the fastest growing religion in Australia. This is one of several mosques in Sydney.

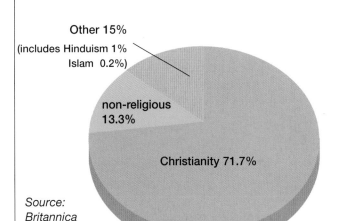

Religions in Australia and Oceania

Other 15%
(includes Hinduism 1%
Islam 0.2%)

non-religious
13.3%

Christianity 71.7%

Source: Britannica Book of the Year 2004

This Aboriginal bark painting depicts the body. It was painted by Lipundja from Milingimbi, Australia.

passed on orally, through dancing, singing, in ceremonies and in forms of visual art. Within Aboriginal spiritual beliefs, every meaningful activity, event or life process that occurs at a particular place leaves behind something of itself, which then shapes some part of the land – rocks, riverbeds, water holes. These places assume significance as 'sacred sites'. Aboriginal culture maintains and adapts the laws that were laid down in the Dreamtime.

ABORIGINAL ART

Traditional Aboriginal art varied enormously throughout Australia, depending on the availability of materials and the practices of each group. Visual representation of Dreamtime stories was made on rocks, on large sheets of bark, and on bodies for ceremonies. Since the 1970s, there has been increasing national and international recognition of the work of contemporary Aboriginal artists. Dreamtime stories are visually told using modern materials, such as canvas and acrylic paint. Aboriginal art and performance has added considerably to Australia's cultural and tourist industries. In addition, sales of artwork have provided Aboriginal communities with a source of income.

CLEVER NATIONS

Australia and New Zealand are often referred to as 'clever nations' because of the literary, artistic and scientific achievements of their small populations. Both nations have vigorous national literature canons, with many authors, such as Nobel prize winner Patrick White from Australia and Janet Frame from New Zealand, receiving international acclaim and prizes. Australia is recognized around the world for its innovation in the fields of agricultural research and biotechnology. Several Australians have won Nobel prizes for scientific advances in medicine, chemistry and physics, and Australian technology is highly competitive internationally.

IN FOCUS: Sport in Australia and New Zealand

Sport is an important social and cultural activity throughout Oceania. Many of the games played were introduced into the region by the British in the nineteenth century. Australia and New Zealand have long enjoyed international recognition for their sporting prowess in a range of sports, including cricket, rugby, swimming, surfing, athletics and tennis. Australia is also the home of its own football code, Australian Rules Football, a game that is based on both Irish and Aboriginal sports 'traditions'. 'Aussie Rules' is a game that relies on excellent ball handling and kicking skills, and great endurance, with players running up to 20-30 kilometres (12-19 miles) during a game.

Australia and New Zealand compete in the 2003 Rugby World Cup series.

35

5. NATURAL RESOURCES IN AUSTRALIA, OCEANIA AND ANTARCTICA

Oceania and Antarctica are rich in natural resources, which have been vigorously sought by individuals, companies and multinational organizations. However this aggressive and, at times, greedy exploitation has often severely damaged the landscapes and natural life of the region.

Wind-driven pumps are used to access sources of water that lie underground.

WATER: THE MOST PRECIOUS RESOURCE

By the end of the nineteenth century most of the land in Australia had been taken by white settlers for grazing, agriculture and mining. Approximately 60 per cent of the Australian continent is used for farming, and most of this is for grazing. In the drier regions, vast grazing properties often stretched over thousands of square kilometres/miles. European farming methods were often unsuitable for the Australian environment, and specialized farming equipment was invented, such as the 'stump-jump plough' which was used to jump over obstacles like old tree stumps and rocks. But the development of Australia's agricultural and grazing industries was dependent on the availability of the continent's most precious resource - water.

Less than 10 per cent of the continent is naturally suitable for growing crops. As a result, around 1.2 million hectares (3 million acres) of cultivated land is under irrigation in Australia,

36

enabling the growth of vegetables, fruit, cotton, and rice. However, irrigation is often costly and drains large amounts of water away from river systems. Cubbie Station in Queensland, for example, relies on the damming of the Condamine-Balonne river system. A giant storage dam is used to irrigate just 14,000 hectares (34,600 acres) of cotton production.

Through intensive grazing and agriculture, settlers have dramatically reshaped and in some cases mismanaged Australia's physical environment. One major problem is soil erosion. Soil erosion is caused by the removal of vegetation by overgrazing, and the damage to the soils by the hooves of cattle and sheep.

In recent decades there has been a growing awareness of the need for water and soil conservation in Australia. Government-sponsored programs have encouraged farmers to plant more trees and care for their land, but the problem of water management remains pressing.

Erosion caused by winds and water run-off is a major environmental problem.

MINERAL AND ENERGY RESOURCES IN AUSTRALIA

Australia is rich in a broad range of natural resources, including bauxite, coal, iron ore, tin, gold, silver, uranium, nickel, tungsten, diamonds, natural gas and petroleum. In 2003-2004, the value of Australia's minerals and energy exports were valued at US$33 billion (31 per cent of export earnings).

The discovery of gold in the 1850s led to the birth of Australia's mining industry. Australia continues to mine about 10 per cent of the world's supply of gold. Heavy machinery and deep tunnels in places such as Kalgoorlie have now replaced the difficult and dangerous work of those early miners. In 2003 gold was worth US$4,534 million as an export commodity and second only to coal (US$8,408 million).

Australia has become the world's largest producer of bauxite, which is used to make aluminium, as well as contributing heavily to the world's supply of iron ore and uranium, a raw material used for generating nuclear power. This extensive mining contributes heavily to Australia's GDP and employment.

Aluminum ore, called bauxite, is most commonly formed in deeply weathered volcanic rocks, usually basalt.

FACT FILE

The discovery of incredibly rich gold deposits at Edie Creek, in Papua New Guinea, in 1926 became one of the biggest alluvial dredging operations in the world.

NATURAL RESOURCES IN OCEANIA

The lure of gold and other raw materials also attracted Europeans into the Pacific. The discovery of gold on New Zealand's South Island in the 1850s boosted the population. Interest in gold mining faded in the 1920s but rising gold prices in the mid 1970s reignited mining investment, exploration and production. Full-scale mining did not begin in New Guinea until the discovery of gold there in the 1880s.

In the 1910s and 1920s chromite mined on New Caledonia constituted 40 per cent of the island's economy and 25 per cent of the world's supply of chromite. In the twenty-first century, mineral riches are being tapped throughout Oceania. Natural gas and oil are found in Papua New Guinea, New Zealand,

Solomon Islands, Vanuatu, Fiji and Tonga; coal, iron ore and hydropower in New Zealand; phosphate in Tonga and Kiribati; cobalt in French Polynesia; and nickel in New Caledonia.

Nauru's legacy of mining phosphate has created a 'moon-like' landscape.

Mining of natural minerals brings much needed foreign currency into the economy of Oceania, but the sustainability of the resource and the effects its exploitation is having on the natural landscape and the lifestyle of local inhabitants have raised considerable environmental and social concerns. On Nauru, phosphate has been mined by German, British and Australian companies throughout the twentieth century, bringing unimagined wealth to its inhabitants. However, the mining of phosphate has removed much of the island's land surface, displacing a traditional agricultural economy. In the process the people of Nauru have become dependent on imports, especially the high sugar and fat content in processed foods leading to alarming rates of diabetes. Forty per cent of Nauru's population of 12,800 people have been diagnosed with diabetes.

FACT FILE

In 2004 the supply of phosphate – the economic base of Nauru – is exhausted, leaving Nauru dependent on Australian aid.

Great tracts of unspoilt rainforests are also being depleted. The debate over unsustainable forests and the clearing of forests for paper products in Australia keeps a political focus on the problem. But elsewhere the concerns of conservationists are largely ignored. The Solomon Islands have already been stripped bare of their forests. A similar fate is now confronting 14 million hectares (34,594,000 acres) of Papua New Guinea. The forests are being harvested by international companies, whose actions are tolerated by the government of Papua New Guinea, because it is desperate

Logging in the Western Province of Papua New Guinea.

for foreign income. The environmental consequences are telling. Runoff from the sawmills and effluent from logging camps are polluting the river systems. There is little regard for traditional hunting and fishing areas, native flora, or burial grounds. The companies are barely providing any infrastructure, and little of the economic benefit is going to the local landowners.

NATURAL RESOURCES IN ANTARCTICA

Early European exploitation of Antarctica was by whalers and sealers. Their rate of fishing soon put whale populations on the brink of extinction. Today commerical fishing interests in Antarctic waters are mostly from Japan and Norway and focus on krill, finfish, cod, herring, and whiting. Once again the amount of fish being taken, especially krill, an essential part of the food chain for whales and other marine species, is raising concern about damage to Antarctica's ecosystem.

Exploration in Antarctica has revealed deposits of iron ore, chromium, copper, gold, nickel, platinum and other minerals, and coal and hydrocarbons have been found in small uncommercial quantities. However, its distance from world markets and its hostile environment has meant that little economic development has taken place. The International Protocol on Environmental Protection to the Antarctic Treaty protects Antarctica from mineral exploitation as well as covering areas of marine pollution until 2050.

• • • • • ▷ IN FOCUS: Mining in Papua New Guinea

In Papua New Guinea, mining accounts for a third of government revenue and 70 per cent of export earnings. The largest source of copper is at the OK Tedi Mine which processes 100,000 tons (90, 720 tonnes) of ore per day. Copper comprises only 1-2 per cent of this ore and the remainder, together with waste rock, is disposed of into rivers, land sites or the ocean. Other environmental damage is caused by the impact of mining on the immediate land – it is estimated that the depth of the open pit at OK Tedi will be 1,300 metres (4,265 feet) by 2010 - as well as the use of land for supporting mining infrastructure, such as processing mills, workshops, accommodation, offices and villages. This environmental damage has had a devastating effect on the traditional culture and agricultural practices of people who live nearby, and it continues to proceed despite their protests.

The OK Tedi copper mine has had serious effects on the environment.

6. THE ECONOMIES OF AUSTRALIA, OCEANIA AND ANTARCTICA

*I*N THE TWENTY-FIRST CENTURY AUSTRALIA IS A HIGHLY industrialized nation with a prosperous Western-style capitalist economy. Its GDP per capita is on a par with dominant West European economies. However, economic development in Oceania has been less bright, and it is severely affected by such factors as size, limited resources, distance from markets and suppliers, and changes in the global economy.

AUSTRALIA'S ECONOMY

From the nineteenth century, the Australian economy has been based on agriculture, especially wool, meat and wheat, and then mining. However, this has changed in the last fifty years, and now the Australian workforce is primarily engaged in secondary production (notably vehicles, medicine and pharmaceuticals, computer and telecommunications equipment) and the service sectors (such as education and tourism).

Aluminium being loaded onto cargo ships for export. Western Australia is one of the world's largest suppliers of aluminium.

Today Australia's main industries are mining (particularly coal, crude petroleum, gold, iron ore and aluminium), manufacturing, agriculture and tourism. Wool remains an important commodity and represents 25 per cent of the world's wool production. Ninety-five per cent of Australian wool is exported to Japan and Europe. Both agricultural products and

44

energy and mineral resources are exported, with Japan (18.5 per cent) and the United States (9.6 per cent) the largest revenue markets. Australia's main imports are machinery and transport equipment, computers and telecommunications components, crude oil and petroleum products. Imports come predominantly from the US (18.3 per cent), Japan (12.3 per cent) and China (10.1 per cent).

Other factors have also contributed to Australia's economic strength. These include increasing trade within its immediate Asia-Pacific region, and the development of new areas of growth, such as tourism. The Australia-United States Free Trade Agreement, negotiated in 2004 with the United States, is also expected to have some positive impact on the economy by eliminating import taxes and encouraging trade between the two countries.

OCEANIA'S ECONOMY

Agriculture, especially dairy products and meat, has been the foundation of New Zealand's economy. Indeed, it has been called 'the largest farm in the world'. Britain has historically been New Zealand's largest trading partner, although new partners have been sought since the 1970s.

By the 1980s New Zealand had reformed its economic base. It is now a heavily industrialized economy with a global market, with interests in food processing, wood and paper products, mining and textiles, as well as a continued reliance on agricultural trade. New Zealand lamb and wool products are recognized internationally for

Sheep on a farm in New Zealand's North Island.

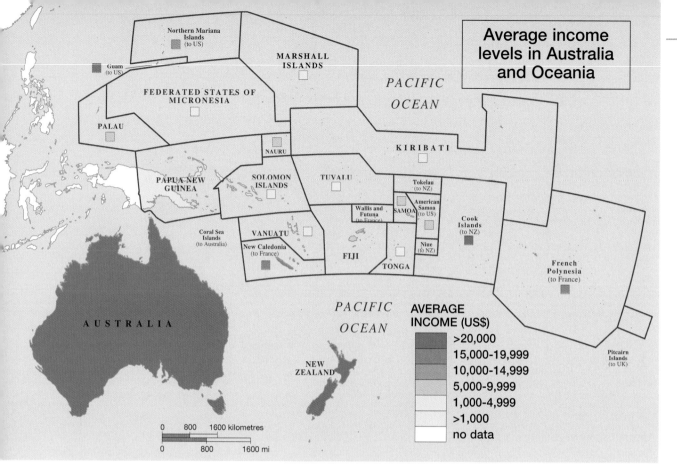

Northern Mariana
Islands
(to US)

Guam
(to US)

MARSHALL
ISLANDS

PACIFIC
OCEAN

FEDERATED STATES OF
MICRONESIA

PALAU

NAURU

KIRIBATI

PAPUA NEW
GUINEA

SOLOMON
ISLANDS

TUVALU

Tokelau
(to NZ)

Wallis and
Futuna
(to France)

SAMOA

American
Samoa
(to US)

Cook
Islands
(to NZ)

Coral Sea
Islands
(to Australia)

VANUATU

New Caledonia
(to France)

FIJI

TONGA

Niue
(to NZ)

French
Polynesia
(to France)

AUSTRALIA

PACIFIC
OCEAN

NEW
ZEALAND

Pitcairn
Islands
(to UK)

**AVERAGE
INCOME (US$)**

>20,000
15,000-19,999
10,000-14,999
5,000-9,999
1,000-4,999
>1,000
no data

0   800   1600 kilometres

0   800   1600 mi

Small landholders such as these Samoan village women are being encouraged to plant high yield crops such as peanuts.

their high quality. Today New Zealand's main export trading partners are Australia (22 per cent), the US (15.6 per cent) and Japan (11.5 per cent).

Most people elsewhere in Oceania continue to live in rural and fishing communities, often in small villages with limited opportunities for employment. The economies of the Oceanic Islands are heavily influenced by ecological factors. Other factors include the availability of arable land, the size of the work force, and the financial potential of each island-nation. Political instability and low foreign investment also play a role in restricting economic growth.

Apart from a small manufacturing sector that primarily processes agricultural products and textiles, subsistence farming and fishing form the bulk of

Oceania's economies. American Samoa has only 5 per cent of arable land along its coastal plains, while Micronesia relies on agriculture for 50 per cent of its domestic economy.

Fiji, with one of the region's most developed economies, is endowed with forests, minerals and fish resources. Yet with only 12 per cent arable land, it still has a large subsistence sector, with 26 per cent of the population under the poverty line. Agriculture (particularly sugar) represents 17 per cent of the economy, industry (small cottage textile industries and larger mining enterprises) represents 25 per cent and services (particularly tourism) another 56 per cent.

The Cook Islands rely economically on agriculture, mainly copra and citrus fruit, and the manufacturing of textiles. Their economic growth is hindered by geographic isolation, the lack of natural resources, and periodic natural disasters such as typhoons. Consequently, the Cook Islands are reliant on foreign aid, particularly from New Zealand and, to a lesser extent, Australia.

Colonial links have been economically useful for some island-nations. French Polynesia has hosted a large French military base since 1962 and has received a large influx of foreign capital. It continues to profit from development agreements with France aimed principally at creating new businesses and strengthening social services. Similarly, American Samoa benefits heavily from its link with the United States.

FACT FILE

In 2003 Australia was the largest provider of foreign aid in Oceania, giving US$352 million to Papua New Guinea and another US$297 million to the Pacific Islands. The money is providing assistance for economic reform and better government administration, education and training, health, and the better management of the environment and natural resources.

The French government has spent millions of $US maintaining its nuclear program in the Pacific.

But dependence on more developed countries is not always beneficial. In 1979 the Federated States of Micronesia fell under United States administration and achieved independence in 1986. As a consequence it has become over-dependent on financial aid from the United States, which has pledged US$3.5 billion (approximately 40 per cent of Micronesia's GDP) between 1986 and 2023. Unemployment is at 16 per cent and 26.7 per cent of its population lives under the poverty line.

TOURISM

The one area of economic growth that is benefiting both Australia and Oceania is tourism. In 2001, when 4.8 million visitors contributed US$13 billion to the Australian economy (11.2 per cent of the total export earnings), the tourism industry employed 6 per cent of Australia's workforce.

Each year growing numbers of tourists from Europe, Australia, Asia and North America visit Oceania. The number of tourists is growing by 10 per cent each year. In 2003 over 1 million people visited the South Pacific Islands alone. The most popular destinations are Fiji, French Polynesia, New Caledonia and Samoa.

Pacific Islands are increasingly focusing on tourism as the basis of their economic development. Smaller nations have been developing niche marketing in adventure, eco and cultural tourism. For some island-nations it is paying, with tourism in North Mariana Islands and Samoa constituting 25 per cent of their economies. Tourism growth across the region, however, is hindered by inadequate air connections and the lack of sufficient facilities such as fresh water and sanitation. Another

FACT FILE

It is anticipated that the number of tourists to Australia will double by 2013.

Western Samoa's Lalomanu Beach is typical of the island paradise that is attracting increasing numbers of tourists to Oceania.

problem is the regular devastation of tourism facilities by extreme climatic occurrences such as cyclones. When Cyclone Ivy hit Vanuatu in February 2004, it disrupted international flights and forced the evacuation of 1,000 residents from the main towns and the closure of some resorts.

Seasonal employment and an economic over-dependence on tourism at the expense of traditional forms of income are some of the detrimental effects of tourism. The economic downturn in Asia during the late 1990s had a major impact on Micronesia, which was very dependent on Asian tourists. Tourism may also present challenges to traditional cultures. Damage to the natural environment by increasing numbers of tourists is a further problem.

FACT FILE

Tourism to Antarctica has become a thriving business with over 13,000 tourists during the 2002-2003 season.

● ● ● ● ▶ IN FOCUS: Tourism in Antarctica

Commercial tourism to Antarctica began in the 1950s, first by cruise ships and then by sightseeing flights from Australia and New Zealand. In 1969 the M/S Lindbald Explorer was the first passenger cruise ship designed specifically for carrying tourists to Antarctica. 'Flight-seeing' or flying at low altitude over Antarctica without landing continues to be popular, despite the 1979 crash of a New Zealand airplane into Mt Erebus, which killed 257 people.

Tourism in Antarctica is controlled by the Protocol on Environmental Protection of the Antarctic Treaty, which was adopted in 1991 to ensure the protection of the environment, and the International Association of Antarctica Tour Operators, who promote safe and environmentally responsible tourism. However, authorities are concerned that they cannot monitor the rapidly increasing rate of tourism and avert ecological damage.

Ecotourists in Antarctica admire Adelie penguins.

7. Australia, Oceania and Antarctica in the World

Most nations in the Pacific region are too small to play a role in world affairs, with the exception of Australia and, to a lesser extent, New Zealand. Yet their history of European colonization has meant that Australia and the island-nations of Oceania have been strongly influenced by the cultures and economies of Europe and the United States.

This relationship with the rest of the world has accelerated since the middle of the twentieth century. During World War II, the military forces of the United States, Australia and New Zealand fought together against Japan in the Pacific. The presence of the Allied and Japanese forces on many Pacific islands was to have an impact on traditional cultures. In Papua New Guinea, in particular, the indigenous population played a key role in assisting Allied troops during the war. In addition, the defence, cultural and economic ties between Australia and the United States were strengthened as a result of the war. In 1951 the

Trading at the Sydney Stock Exchange.

FACT FILE

The Australian trading day on the stock market is truly global – it spans the close of business in the United States and the opening of business in Europe, and coincides with business in Asia.

regional defence ANZUS Treaty was signed between Australia, New Zealand and the United States, signalling a new era of international relations within the region.

Today, the impact of global trade and the influence of global media have meant that the cultures and economies of these nations are increasingly bound up in worldwide developments.

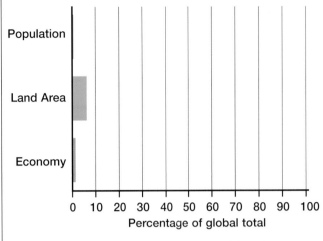

Australia, Oceania and Antarctica compared with the rest of the world

Percentage of global total

Source: United Nations; World Bank; Britannica Book of the Year 2004

AUSTRALIA AND NEW ZEALAND AND THE WORLD

Australia's international relations were traditionally linked to those of Britain, but after 1945 its security in the region has been increasingly aligned with the United States. Australian forces have played a role in international conflicts in Korea, Vietnam, the Gulf War and Iraq. They have also been involved in United Nations peace-keeping activities, including playing a leading role in East Timor.

Australia's engagement with the world has also been increasingly concerned with the region of Asia, especially in relation to trade. Between 1983 and 2002, foreign investment in Australia grew from US$63,388 million to US$177,540 million, of which 28.7 per cent came from American sources and 10.4 per cent from Japanese, Hong Kong and Chinese sources.

Australia has taken on a leading role within the Pacific region, particularly in ensuring political and economic stability. It is the major provider of foreign aid and assistance programmes to the

More than 1000 Australian troops and civilians helped in the rebuilding of East Timor after it gained independence from Indonesia in 2002.

The Sydney Olympics were watched by an additional 1.2 million tourists as athletes from over 100 countries competed.

underdeveloped countries in the region. Australian aid includes funds for educational, health and economic development programmes.

Like Australia, New Zealand was historically linked to Britain and its foreign policy, but more recently has given priority to its immediate region. New Zealand has been a strong opponent of nuclear testing by the United States in the Pacific. As a consequence of this objection, New Zealand withdrew from active participation in the ANZUS Treaty in 1986. New Zealand is an important member in Pacific-wide economic and cultural organizations and developments.

Tourism to New Zealand is also growing, and the country's scenic beauty and developed infrastructure has made it a desirable and highly competitive location for international film production. Peter Jackson's 'Lord of the Rings' films have given New Zealand an international profile.

ANTARCTICA AND THE WORLD
The Antarctic Treaty signed on 1 December 1959 established the legal framework for the management of Antarctica. Today there are 45 treaty member nations. Consultative, or voting,

members include the seven nations that claim portions of Antarctica as national territory (Argentina, Australia, Chile, New Zealand, the United Kingdom, France and Norway) and 20 non-claimant nations. Antarctica is administered through meetings of the consultative member nations. Decisions from these meetings are carried out by these member nations (within their areas) in accordance with their own national laws.

INTERNATIONAL CHALLENGES

In recent years, the 'War against Terror' has been fought on numerous fronts across the Asia-Pacific region. Terrorist bombings were directed against Australia in 2002, when many Australian vacationers were killed in an attack on a nightclub in Bali in Indonesia. The Australian Embassy in Jakarta was also bombed in 2004. As a consequence, Australian authorities are co-operating internationally to monitor and prevent terrorist activities.

Enforcement agencies in Australia and New Zealand are concerned over the region's increasing problems in enforcing the control of national borders and preventing illegal immigration. The policing of illegal immigration in the region involves co-operation with authorities in Asia, Europe and the United States. There are also growing concerns over the increasing incidence of crime in the Pacific region, including the trafficking of illegal drugs. Again, the regional responses to these activities have been conducted in association with international law-enforcement bodies.

ENVIRONMENTAL ISSUES IN A GLOBAL CONTEXT

Climate change is a global phenomenon with lasting and adverse consequences. It has been predicted that because of the delicate and unique environments of Australia and Oceania the effect of climate change will particularly affect the economic developments within the region. There is concern that the

The Australian Navy clears mines from Umm Qasr Port in Iraq in March 2003.

FACT FILE

The Pacific Ocean contains other island-nations that are not part of Oceania. Indonesia, the Philippines and Japan are located in the continent of Asia. The islands that lie in the eastern Pacific Ocean near North America and South America are parts of those continents. The nations that border the Pacific Ocean are referred to as part of the Pacific Rim.

increased melting of the polar ice-caps, which will lead to rising sea levels, poses a long-term threat to small island-nations in Oceania and the coastal areas of Australia and New Zealand.

The United Nations Framework on Climate Change has established the Kyoto Protocol, which aims to reduce the amount of greenhouse gases that are emitted through the use of energy, in industry and agriculture, and the use of motor vehicles. New Zealand has ratified the Kyoto Protocol and its government is committed to environmentally sustainable policies. Australia, like the United States, has not ratified the Kyoto Protocol, but has allocated funding to reduce the emission of greenhouse gases and to develop new and efficient environmentally sensitive technologies.

The Pacific Islands Forum aims to enhance the economic and social well being of the peoples of the South Pacific by cooperation between governments and international agencies.

REGIONAL CO-OPERATION

The nations of Oceania have united to represent their broad interests in international affairs. The Pacific Islands Forum (formerly the South Pacific Forum 1971-2000) meets annually to discuss regional trade and security. In 2003 the Forum voted to intervene in the Solomon Islands where significant deterioration of law and order was threatening the stability of the community. Since 1994 the Forum has had observer status at the United Nations and at meetings of the Asia-Pacific Economic Cooperation (APEC).

APEC was founded in 1989 to assist economic growth in the Asia-Pacific region. It has 21 'member economies' which include Australia, New Zealand and Papua New Guinea as well as the United States, Japan, the People's Republic of China and other nations in the Pacific Rim and Asia. Together, these member economies account for almost 50 per cent of the world's trade and over one-third of the world's population.

Other regional organizations include the South Pacific Commission, established in 1947 by European powers with interests in Oceania to provide development assistance, the Tourism Council of the South Pacific, and the South Pacific Regional Environment Program. Another 200 regional organizations link interests across business, the arts, communications and education.

•••••• ▷ IN FOCUS: Nuclear testing

One of the strongest co-operative developments has been the response to nuclear testing in the South Pacific. First the Americans in the 1950s, then the French until the 1980s, tested nuclear weapons at remote atolls over which they had possession. In August 1985 eight members of the South Pacific Forum signed the Treaty of Raratonga, requiring all nations to stop testing or storing nuclear weapons in the South Pacific, and from dumping nuclear waste there. The major nuclear powers had signed and ratified the protocols by 1997.

Greenpeace's ship 'Rainbow Warrior', used in anti-nuclear protests, was sabotaged with bombs by French spies on 10 July 1985. One crew member drowned.

8. WILDLIFE IN AUSTRALIA, OCEANIA AND ANTARCTICA

*T*HE GEOLOGICAL SEPARATION OF LANDMASSES AND THE ISOLATED processes of species evolution over millions of years have resulted in the region's diversity of unique flora and fauna.

Grey kangaroos can jump up to 9 metres (30 feet) in a single bound.

FACT FILE

Kangaroos are a protected species, but annual assessments determine whether legal harvesting is necessary to maintain their numbers at a sustainable level.

ANIMAL LIFE

Australia's unique fauna include monotremes (egg-laying mammals) like the platypus and echidna. Also found only in Australia is the dingo, a large hunting dog that came from Asia to Australia approximately 5,000 years ago. Among the 16 marsupial families native to Australia are possums, tree-dwelling koalas, wombats, kangaroos and wallabies. There are 50 species of kangaroo in Australia, the largest being the grey and red kangaroos. The population of kangaroos in 2003 was approximately 28 million (90 per cent were the red and grey kangaroos).

More than 360 of Australia's 750 vibrant bird species are unique to the continent. Australia's largest native bird, the emu, stands 2 metres (6.5 feet) tall and is found throughout the continent. Also distinct to Australia are honeyeaters, bowerbirds and frogmouths and an array of 50 species of brilliantly coloured parrots. These include parakeets, lorikeets, cockatoos and galahs. Australian customs authorities guard against the illegal smuggling of live parrots out of the country.

Flightless Kagu birds in the rainforests of New Caledonia.

The absence of land dwelling mammals from New Zealand and other parts of Oceania allowed the evolution of a diversified range of exotic birds. A number of these birds are flightless, because they had no need to fly away from predators. These include the kakapos, kiwis and moas (now extinct) in New Zealand, and New Caledonia's forest-dwelling kagu. New Guinea's extraordinarily plumed 'bird of paradise' lives in the lowland and mid-mountain forests. Its spectacular colours serve as attractors during mating season and also function as protective camouflage amidst the colours of the forest.

Marine mammals, including several species of whales and dolphins, are common in the waters of the Pacific Ocean. In New Zealand and Australia, 'whale watching' has become an important tourist attraction. There are also many species of sharks. Sometimes these pose dangers to swimmers and surfers, so a 'shark patrol' operates on many popular Australian beaches, calling all to shore when sharks are sighted.

PLANT LIFE

Some of Australia and New Zealand's flora are also remnants of Gondwanaland. Huge kauri and southern beech, broad-leaf evergreens and conifers are found in the dense rainforests of New Zealand. The rainforests of

FACT FILE

Of the 20,000 species of plants in Australia, 17,000 are unique to the continent. Eighty to ninety per cent of all mammals, insects and reptiles in Australia are also found nowhere else on Earth.

FACT FILE

Australia has more poisonous snakes than any other continent. The most venomous snake in the world, the Eastern Taipan, lives in the desert interior.

New Zealand's kauri are among the world's greatest trees, reaching heights of 50 metres (164 feet).

Northern Queensland contain flowering plants, palms and laurels, and more than 500 species of eucalyptus while the temperate rainforests of Tasmania have myrtle beech, tree ferns and moss.

CONSERVATION

In Australia and New Zealand conservation of natural environments and of plant and animal species has been aided by international organizations, such as Greenpeace, as well as national government and non-government organizations. Community protest has drawn attention to conservation issues, and was successful in preventing the damming of the Franklin River in Tasmania in the 1980s. There are now many national parks in Australia and New Zealand. Classified World Heritage sites in Australia include national parks at Uluru/Ayers Rock and at Kakadu in the Northern Territory.

WILDLIFE IN ANTARCTICA

Each season about 100 million birds breed around Antarctica's coastline and offshore islands including species of petrels, terns and the wandering albatross. Four species of penguin are found on Antarctica. During winter, male Emperor penguins, their bodies protected by a thick layer of insulating fat, huddle together in a large group to keep the eggs, that they balance on their feet, warm.

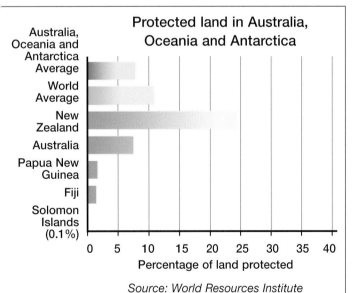

Protected land in Australia, Oceania and Antarctica

Percentage of land protected

Australia, Oceania and Antarctica Average
World Average
New Zealand
Australia
Papua New Guinea
Fiji
Solomon Islands (0.1%)

0 5 10 15 20 25 30 35 40

Source: World Resources Institute

The huge hole in the ozone layer over Antarctica, caused by global warming, is already endangering wildlife. Icebergs are breaking away from the coast of Antarctica and preventing colonies of more than 100,000 penguins from reaching their breeding grounds. Scientists fear that the Adelie penguins in the southern part of the Ross Sea will not survive.

Despite the extreme climate, a surprising number of plants thrive in Antarctica, particularly the many species of lichen, mosses and fungi, and over 700 species of algae.

Adelie penguins find food in the open waters of the Antarctic.

●●●●▶ IN FOCUS: The Great Barrier Reef

The Great Barrier Reef lies off the coast of Queensland, Australia. It is made up of many tiny organisms called coral polyps joined together by their outer skeletons. The Reef is home to 1,500 species of brilliantly coloured tropical fish and 400 types of hard and soft coral. Coral bleaching is increasing, as are predators, such as poisonous crown-of-thorns starfish. Since the 1960s, nesting loggerhead turtles have declined by 50-80 per cent while the dugong (a marine mammal that lives mainly on plants and is also known as a sea cow) populations are nearly extinct. Humans are the Reef's greatest threat. Recreational divers who harm coral, pollution, and fishing with chemicals, or the use of explosives to increase a catch, all pose threats. In July 2004, however, the Great Barrier Reef was declared a Maritime National Park, effectively ending commercial fishing on large sections of the Reef.

The coral and marine life of the Great Barrier Reef attracts thousands of divers annually.

9. THE FUTURE OF AUSTRALIA, OCEANIA AND ANTARCTICA

*T*HERE ARE MANY IMMEDIATE AND LONG-TERM CHALLENGES FOR Australia, Oceania and Antarctica during the twenty-first century. The role of regional and international co-operation is increasingly important. The remote nations of the Pacific, while maintaining their unique identities, are now part of global economic and cultural processes.

REGIONAL STABILITY

Both Australia and New Zealand have stable economies and political systems, and are keen to promote stability within the wider region. Most Pacific island-nations have achieved independence from former colonial governments. Democratic systems of government have been adopted by these nations, but in many cases there is pressure for further political reform from younger generations. This pressure has highlighted social divisions and may conflict with traditional systems of social hierarchy and chiefly rule. In Papua New Guinea and New Caledonia there has been political unrest as particular ethnic groups have sought independence from the ruling government.

Foreign aid has been critical for the economic stability of many Oceanic nations. While Australia is the major contributor of foreign aid in the Pacific, the emphasis remains on sustainable development and the need to develop new and ongoing sources of revenue.

On 2 April 2000, 80,000 plastic 'hands' were planted in the sands of Sydney's Coogee Beach to show support by Australians for reconciliation between Indigenous and non-Indigenous Australians.

Other issues such as the adequate provision of education, housing and health services, and the demands of the labour market require attention. So does the problem of widespread poverty in many underdeveloped Oceanic islands. In wealthy countries such as Australia, the gap between those on higher and lower incomes is widening.

Increases in population have created an urgent problem for some Oceanic nations where land and resources are limited. However, the situation is different in Australia and New Zealand where both countries have a low birth rate and the population is growing older. Here, the economic and social implications are serious, including rising costs to governments in providing 'old age' pensions. The number of immigrants allowed into Australia each year remains widely debated. So too does the question of the rights and needs of Australia's and New Zealand's indigenous peoples.

While scientists continue to explore Antarctica, international disputes over territorial claims by various nations with direct and indirect interests remain a preoccupation of the members of the Antarctic Treaty.

Increasing costs of living are forcing Australian retirees back into the workforce and placing a strain on the government provision of pensions and heath facilities.

THE ULTIMATE CHALLENGE

The management of the environment looms as the greatest challenge facing Antarctica, Australia and Oceania. Long-term concerns include pollution, the depletion of the ozone layer and its climatic consequences, and the over-exploitation of the region's rich resources. The control of environmental damage by introduced species, and the need to halt the possible extinction of many species of plant and animal life in the region also needs addressing.

STATISTICAL COMPENDIUM

*** Data from 2000
Sources: UN Agencies, World Bank,
Social Watch and Britannica

Nation	Area (sq km)	Population (2003)	Urbanization (% population) 2003	Life expectancy at birth 2002 (in years)	GDP per capita (US $) 2002	Percentage of population under 15 years 2003	Percentage of population over 65 years 2003
American Samoa	199	62,000	90.3	N/a	N/a	N/a	N/a
Australia	7,682,300	19,731,000	92	79.1	28,260	20	12
Fiji	18,272	839,000	51.7	69.6	5,440	33	4
French Polynesia	4,000	244,000	52.1	74.0	28,020***	30	6
Guam	541	163,000	93.7	78.0	N/a	34	7
Kiribati	811	88,000	47.3	63.0	N/a	39	3
Marshall Islands	181	53,000	66.3	65.0***	N/a	N/a	N/a
Micronesia	701	109,000	29.3	69.0	N/a	36	4
Nauru	21.2	13,000	100.0	N/a	N/a	N/a	N/a
New Caledonia	18,576	228,000	61.2	74.0	25,200***	29	7
New Zealand	270,534	3,875,000	85.9	78.2	21,740	22	12
Northern Mariana Islands	477	79,000	94.2	N/a	N/a	N/a	N/a
Palau	488	20,000	68.6	70.0***	N/a	N/a	N/a
Papua New Guinea	462,840	5,711,000	13.2	57.4	2,270	41	2
Samoa	2,831	178,000	22.3	69.8	5,600	35	5
Solomon Islands	28,370	477,000	16.5	69.0	1,590	45	3
Tonga	750	104,000	33.4	68.4	6,850	33	9
Tuvalu	25.6	11,000	55.2	N/a	N/a	N/a	N/a
Vanuatu	12,190	212,000	22.8	68.6	2,890	41	3

GLOSSARY

Aboriginal Indigenous peoples of Australia.

Adaro A Melanesian mythical creature that is half human and half fish. It lives in the sun and travels to earth on rainbows.

Allied Nations that agree to fight on the same side.

Alluvial Gold bearing soil.

Alluvial plains A flat area built up over many thousands of years by deposits of river sediment, such as a delta or estuary.

Amalgamated Joined together.

Artesian A reservoir of water lying under the earth's surface.

Atoll A coral lagoon where a ring-shaped coral reef encloses a lagoon.

Bauxite Aluminium ore that is found in deeply weathered volcanic rock.

Canon In literature, a body of books that are widely recognised.

Climate change The process of long-term changes to the world's climate.

Continental shelf An area of seabed between the shore of a continent and the deeper ocean.

Coral The skeleton of sea animals that collectively form reefs and, sometimes, islands.

Coral bleaching The loss of colour in the coral caused by the loss of microscopic plants that live in the coral and provide the coral with food for growth.

Dominion A territory subject to the control of another nation.

Dormant A volcano that is inactive.

Dredging Removal of earth (from a river etc) for processing.

Effluent The flow from a stream, or drainage, into the sea.

Emu A flightless Australian bird.

Erosion The wearing away of a substance, such as soil, from wind and/or water.

Federated United in a league or political organization with a central government and a number of separate states that maintain control of their internal affairs.

GDP (Gross Domestic Product) The market value of all goods and services produced within a country over a set period of time.

Geographic South Pole The point where the earth's axis of rotation intersects the surface.

Greenhouse gases Atmospheric gases, such as carbon dioxide and methane, that trap some of the heat radiating from the Earth's surface. Greenhouse gases contribue to global warming and climate change.

Gondwanaland An ancient land mass in the Southern Hemisphere that broke up about 600 million years ago to form Antarctica, South America, Africa and Australia.

Indentured A person who was brought from another country to work for a period of time.

Indian sub-continent The peninsula of South Asia that takes in India, Bangladesh, Pakistan and Sri Lanka.

Indigenous Native to a particular geographical area.

Infrastructure Networks that allow communication and/or help people and the economy to function. Examples include roads, railways, electricity and phone lines.

Irrigation The artificial watering of soil.

Kinship The network of family relations.

Krill The common name to some 85 species of small free-swimming crustaceans called euphausiids.

Magnetic South Pole The point where the field line of the earth's magnetic field points directly into the earth. Here the compass points north. The Magnetic South Point is located in the Antarctic Ocean.

Maori Indigenous peoples of New Zealand

Marsupial A type of mammal who carries and suckles its newly born in a stomach pouch on the outside of the body.

Missionaries People who are sent to another place to spread a religion or do social work.

Monsoon The season when winds bring heavy rains.

Outcroppings Part of a rock formation that appears above the surface of the surrounding land or sea.

Penal colony A prison (or jail), often on an island from which it is difficult to escape, where prisoners are exiled.

Ratified The formal approval of an agreement, such as a treaty.

Salinity The remains of salt deposits in the soil that depletes its agricultural usefulness.

Solar radiation The amount of radiation or energy received from the sun at any given point.

Spinifex A stiff-leaved plant found in Australia's arid conditions.

Further information

Books to read:

Australia and Antarctica: Island Continents by Bruce McClish (Heinemann Library, 2003)

Changing Face of Australia by Margot Richardson (Hodder Wayland, 2003)

Countries of the World: Australia by Robert Prosser (Evans, 2004)

Culture in Papua New Guinea by Melanie Guile (Heinemann, 2003)

Culture in New Zealand by Melanie Guile (Heinemann, 2003)

Life in the Freezer: Natural History of the Antarctic by David Attenborough (Foreword), et al, (BBC Books, 1994)

Useful websites:

www.70south.com/home
Up-to-date news reports on matters relating to Antarctica.

www.gbrmpa.gov.au/index.html
This government website provides an enormous amount of information and pictures of the Great Barrier Reef.

www.mpi.org.au/
This site is run by the Mineral Policy Institute, Australia, and is dedicated to campaigning and research to prevent environmentally and socially destructive mining, minerals and energy projects in Australia, Asia and the Pacific.

www.govt.nz/en/aboutnz/
This government site has lots of information and links about New Zealand.

www.odci.gov/cia/publications/factbook/
Offers the CIA facts and figures on every country.

INDEX

ABOUT THE AUTHOR

Kate Darian-Smith is Professor of Australian Studies and History at the University of Melbourne, Australia. She is the Director of the Australian Centre, an interdisciplinary research and teaching department which focuses on Australia's human and natural environments within their international context. Kate has previously taught in universities in the UK and the USA. She is the author and editor of several books on Australian history and society, including a number of books written for young people about Australia and the Asia-Pacific region.